The Old Things

Diana Noonan

Gran was moving to a small house.
She could not take all her old things.

Gran sent an email to Tom.
She wanted to give him her old things.

To Tom

From Gran

Send

Dear Tom,

This is my record player.

It is very old!

I played music on it.

Would you like it?

Love,

Gran

To
Gran
From
Tom
Send
Dear Gran,
I play music on my MP3 player.
I would like your record player, too.
Thank you.
Love,
Tom
PS Do you have some records
to play on it?
MENU

To Tom

From Gran

Send

Dear Tom,

This is my old camera.

You will need film to take
a photo with it.

Would you like it?

Love,

Gran

Dear Gran,

Thank you, but we have a camera.

It shows a photo as soon as you take it.

Bye,

Tom

To: Tom

From: Gran

Send

Dear Tom,

This is my typewriter.

It is very old!

I typed letters on it.

Would you like it?

Love,

Gran

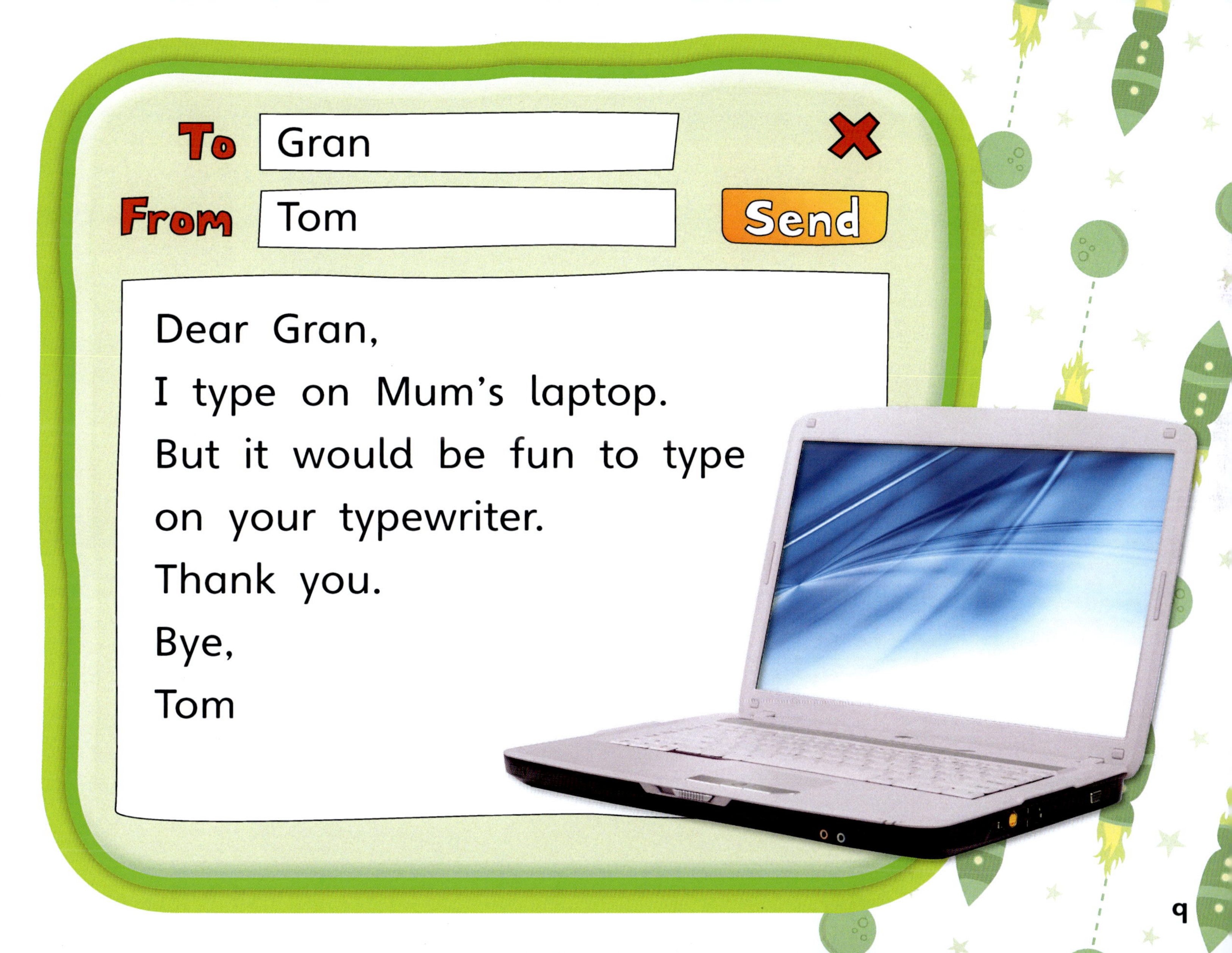
To
Gran
From
Tom
Send
Dear Gran,
I type on Mum's laptop.
But it would be fun to type
on your typewriter.
Thank you.
Bye,
Tom

To Tom

From Gran

Send

Dear Tom,

This is my dad's telephone.

It is very old!

Would you like it?

Love,

Gran

To Gran

From Tom

Dear Gran,

Thank you, but I cannot use your old phone!

But I can ring you on Dad's mobile phone.

Love,

Tom

PS Dad's mobile phone is so small!

To Tom

From Gran

Send

Dear Tom,

Here are my old pen and ink pot.

I used them at school.

I want to give them to you.

Love,

Gran

To Gran
From Tom
Send
Dear Gran,
Thank you for the pen and ink pot.
At school, I use these pencils.
Love,
Tom
PS How will you get
the old things
to my house?

To Tom

From Gran

Send

Dear Tom,

I will put the old things in a box.

I will post them.

There was post when I was a girl.

There is still post now.

Some things stay the same!

Love,

Gran

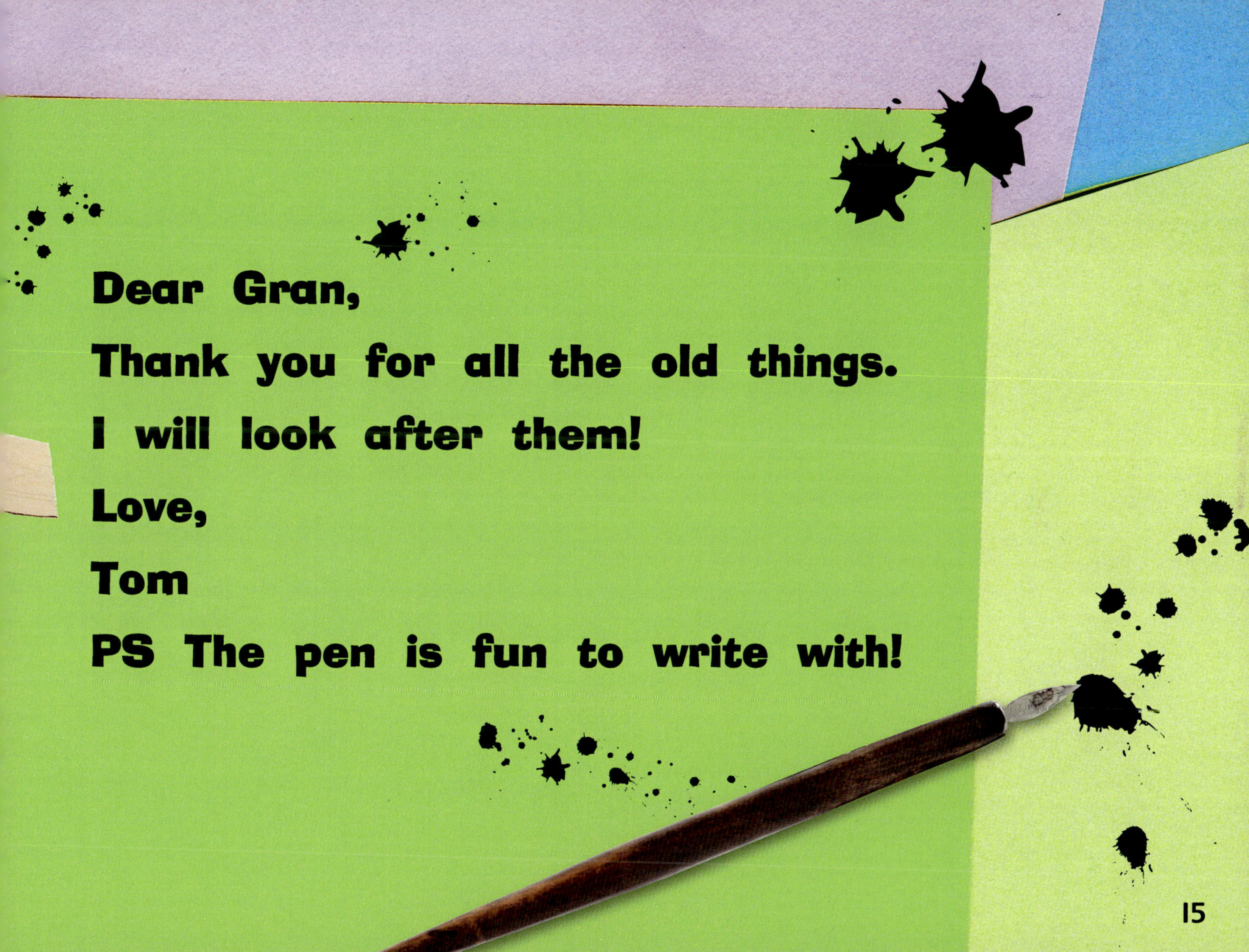

Dear Gran,

Thank you for all the old things.

I will look after them!

Love,

Tom

PS The pen is fun to write with!

BACK THEN

BACK THEN	TODAY
 record player	MP3 player 
camera	digital camera 
 typewriter	 
telephone	mobile phone 
pen and ink	pencils